The Wisdom

of the

Rooms

Volume Four

The Wisdom of the Rooms, **Volume Four** speaks to core, common issues that people with addiction struggle with, and explains them in understandable, humble and enlightening reflections. The honest insights (triggered by quotes and sayings often shared in recovery circles) are tinged with wisdom. Michael's willingness to share openly about his regrettable behaviors, and how he continued to grow in spite of himself, will serve as a light raised in a dark passageway, letting others see themselves, and ultimately to forgive and love themselves. Highly recommended for those wishing to deepen their understanding and experience of recovery."

-- Kelly Madigan Erlandson, LADC, Author, Getting Sober: A Practical Guide to Making it Through the First 30 Days

The Wisdom of the Rooms is a delightful book, which can be read many times over. Michael Z introduces the reader to a bouquet of interesting quotes and sayings assembled from his wide range of exposure to the addiction recovery field. Readers are encouraged to pick and choose his or her way through various quotes by using the reflection questions which help deepen their insight. The Wisdom of the Rooms makes a great addition to the recovery library.

-- Barbara Sinor, Ph.D., Author, Tales of Addiction and Inspiration for Recovery

I regularly share these passages with my patients in our morning groups at Sierra Tucson, and they consistently relate to them and ask for copies. Thank you for your fine service, Michael Z. Keep up the good work!

-- Phillip S. Mitchell, M.A., MFT (CA), MAC, Primary Therapist, Lecturer, Sierra Tucson Treatment Center

The weekly *Wisdom of the Rooms* has become a huge tool in my recovery. The messages are simple and always hit home, and for whatever reason they are usually timely in regards to where I am in my recovery. Again, thank you for sharing The Wisdom of the Rooms. Here is something I heard in my early recovery that helped me learn to share: "A sorrow shared is half a sorrow, and a joy shared is doubled." God bless.

-- Ken L, Grateful Recovery Compulsive Gambler

I just started reading *The Wisdom of the Rooms* and loved it so much that a group of friends and I are using it as a book study. Although I've been around the "rooms" for almost 23 years, there are some sayings I've never heard, and Michael's explanation of the ones I have heard are enlightening. Someone once told me when I first came around to always remain teachable. The Wisdom of the Rooms continues to teach me and open up new doors to my recovery, which I welcome with open arms. I am trying to become the person God wants me to be.

-- Mickey R.

I bought *The Wisdom of the Rooms, Volume One* and have kept it in the car for those moments where I need some good recovery reading. Traffic jams, and those emergency "Life on life's terms" moments we all have. No matter where I am, the quotes, thoughts and readings fill me up with good things to consider. This is an excellent resource to add to your recovery library. We're all in it together. Thanks Michael Z, for adding to my tool kit!

Keeping it simple, one day at a time,

-- Greta L.

I always look forward to Mondays because I know that I will receive a new quote from *The Wisdom of the Rooms*. Over the years, these Wisdom quotes have given me insight into my faulty thinking patterns, courage to face my fears, and tools to adopt a healthier, addiction-free life. I am so thankful to Michael Z for reaching out to others and giving them a helping hand to pull them out of their pain.

-- Nancy H.

I use *The Wisdom of the Rooms* as a tool where I volunteer at a treatment center. There have been times when there seems to be a central issue in the group, and these serve as an objective point of view that I can offer, rather than "I deal/dealt with it this way." The women respond very well. I, too, attach great value to them in my own recovery. There are days when I click into one of these and it's like an answer to what I've asked my Higher Power to help with . . . and that may be just what it is!

-- Valerie

Volume Four

The Wisdom of the Rooms

A Year of Weekly Reflections

Michael Z

Palm Tree Press
Orlando

Palm Tree Press

Published by Palm Tree Press
Printed in the United States of America

Volume Four
First Edition

ISBN-13: 978-1-935602-08-8

To all the people who have come before me and who continue to trudge the road of happy destiny. It is your experience, strength and hope that continue to inspire me.

Table of Contents

Table of Contents

Table of Contents

Table of Contents

Foreword

An ancient proverb says that "Wisdom is more precious than rubies; nothing you desire can compare with her." I have found this to be true in my own journey of recovery over the past few decades, and I've also found the series of books *The Wisdom of the Rooms* by Michael Z to be superb sources of wisdom—resources that can help change lives.

If you or someone you know has struggled (or is struggling) with substance abuse, then these books are a must-read. Anyone who is familiar with the array of challenges involved in beginning the journey of recovery knows that this is a high-maintenance problem—a problem that can be conquered, but one that needs daily attention.

People in recovery, and also those who surround them, need encouragement to hang in there, one day at a time. They also need help knowing how others in sobriety have learned to cope with everyday issues. This is what I see in Michael's books. Michael has a gift—to take the complicated and distill it into short nuggets of wisdom.

As a Prison Chaplain for seventeen years and a person in longtime recovery myself, I have facilitated hundreds of 12-Step meetings (both to the incarcerated as well as the community at large). A few years ago, I started using excerpts and stories from Volumes One, Two and Three of this series as topics of discussion in these meetings.

The Boulder County Jail (Boulder, Colorado) has a therapeutic community in one of its housing units called "The Phoenix Project." I conducted weekly recovery meetings for the men in this section of the jail. After many years facilitating these meetings, I find I need fresh ideas for discussion topics. The Wisdom of the Rooms series has become one of my favorite such resources.

I was shocked to receive a most unusual response after one of the first times I used an excerpt as the meeting discussion topic (Volume One, page 64: If nothing changes, nothing changes). At the conclusion of this particular meeting, the entire group gave a resounding applause! As much as I would love to take credit for this, I must say that the topic of discussion spoke to these men in a way that clearly resonated deeply.

Another excerpt that has been especially meaningful to those who are incarcerated and their families is from Volume Three: page 88: God will never give you more than you can handle—but life will. This topic has been the perfect segue to discussing Steps One, Two and Three.

These valuable topics bring about thoughts and discussions that often only occur in the midst of a 12-Step meeting. Some of my other most-successful topics for meeting discussions include such Wisdom Quotes as: I know I have another drunk in me, but I don't know if I have another recovery; The only thing that can ever make me drink again is untreated alcoholism; and Did God introduce me to the program, or did the program introduce me to God?

Over the past few years, I've recommended these books to other Chaplains in the Denver area, especially if they have no personal history or experience with alcohol or substance abuse. There is much to be gleaned from the pages of these books for both those in the professional treatment world, as well as the non-professional reader.

I consider *The Wisdom of the Rooms* series of books to be one of the top resources for those who genuinely seek to gain and maintain a life of sobriety and serenity. This much-anticipated fourth volume in the series continues to deliver brilliant new insights that often can be found only within the walls of the program meetings. Those who have not had the privilege to attend these12-step meetings rarely have the opportunity to benefit from listening to these nuggets of wisdom. Few people have the ability to gather and rewrite these insights in a way that speaks to the reader's heart as well as Michael Z.

Keep this book on your nightstand so you can begin and end your day with hope and encouragement. Not only will you be glad you did, but those close to you will benefit as well.

I'm convinced that it is God's will that every man and woman who is genuinely seeking a life of complete sobriety be victorious. This book is one more powerful tool to help make this a reality,

and to give insight to the friends and family struggling to help
and to understand. Bravo, Michael! Keep up the good work you
do—because wisdom really is precious.

Your good friend in Colorado,

Joe Herzanek
Former Chaplain: Boulder County Jail (Boulder, Colorado)
Author, Why Don't They Just Quit? What families and
friends need to know about addiction and recovery.
Speaker/Certified Addiction Professional
President, Changing Lives Foundation

Introduction

I will never forget the first quote I heard in recovery, or the impact it had on me. I was several months sober and still emerging from the fog of my addiction, and I was sitting in a small meeting room in North Hollywood with my sponsor. The speaker had seven years of sobriety – which seemed like an impossible feat to me – and he was talking about what he called the one important element needed to get and maintain sobriety: Change. To explain this, he said simply, "The same man will drink again."

When I heard that quote, I didn't know what he meant. After the meeting, I talked to my sponsor about it, and he told me that if I wasn't willing to change, then I would likely keep drinking and using. What I didn't understand was what he meant by "Change." "Change what?" I asked. My sponsor looked at me with his mischievous grin and said, "Michael, you only need to change one thing, and that's everything."

As I worked and worked the steps, and peeled back the endless layers of my personality, I kept finding more aspects of myself that needed changing. It was difficult at first to let go of attitudes, beliefs and behaviors I used to get what I thought I needed, but little by little, I was able to discard them. Some were easier to let go of than others. Sometimes I held on to things far too long, and other times I even went back to old patterns. Eventually though, I found that the more I changed, the less tolerance I had for my old ways and my old self. At some point, I became a new person to whom drinking and using were no longer an option, and when that happened, I finally understood what the speaker had meant all those years ago.

A lot has changed since that early day in my recovery, and throughout it all, I've listened to and been guided by the hundreds of quotes and sayings I've heard in meeting rooms around the world. The wisdom in these quotes transcend individual experience and point to a deeper reservoir, a collective experience, that help us make sense of the journey and of ourselves. I am eternally grateful to all those who have come before me and who have given us so much experience, strength and hope. And I am especially grateful for all the wisdom in the rooms...

Month One

Week One

"When I wake up in the morning, 80% of the things in my head are none of my business."

I don't know about you, but some mornings when I wake up, I'm so overwhelmed with what I'm thinking that I can barely get out of bed. "What if I don't make enough money this week?" "What's going to happen if the economy tanks again and in six months I have to sell my home?" "What if my sore throat turns out to be cancer?" On and on I go until I'm frozen with fear and defeated before I even begin the day.

When I heard today's quote, it was explained to me that what's going to happen a week or even two days from now is none of my business. My job is to suit up and show up today, do the very best I can, and then turn the results over to God. I learned that I have absolutely no control over the future, but I do have control over the actions I take today, and this is where my energy and focus needs to be.

While I sometimes find this hard to practice, I always find that when I do, my day and my life goes much better. First of all, action is the answer to all my fears. Just doing something - anything - instantly makes me feel better. Second, God does exist, He's working in my life, and He's never let me down. Just spending five minutes in the morning in meditation remembering this changes my entire day.

And once I clear out 80% of the thoughts that are none of my business, it's easy to focus on the 20% that make up my life on any given day.

Reflections:

Am I ever overwhelmed by thoughts when I wake up in the morning?

What percentages of them are about the future or about other people, places and things that I have no control over?

How much of the time do I focus in on the actions that I can take today?

Do I spend my mornings in prayer and meditation?

What happens to me when I do?

How do I feel once I begin taking action?

Week Two

"If I'm OK with me, I have no need to make you wrong."

One of the biggest gifts I've been given in recovery is the ability to pause when I'm feeling anxious, angry or judgmental and ask myself what I'm afraid of. Just today as I was driving, I found that I was taking all the other driver's inventories. That guy was driving too fast; she was making an illegal U-turn; that guy was driving like an idiot and should be locked up. Suddenly a wonderful awareness came over me and I stopped and did a quick fear inventory. Within minutes I was restored to sanity, and once again my focus was where it should have been - on my own driving.

It didn't always used to be this way. For years whenever I was feeling out of sorts, I looked outside of myself for the cause. There was always someone not doing things my way, or someone acting worse than I was, and it was easy to point out their faults to make myself feel better. Needless to say, I had more resentments than friends, and when I entered the program I was angry and alone.

What I've learned in recovery is that whenever I'm feeling irritable, restless or discontented, it is always because I'm in self-centered fear and spiritually disconnected from my Higher Power. The ability to recognize this has literally changed my life, and today I use the tools of the program to self-soothe and to live comfortably in my own skin.

Today if I'm OK with me, I have no need to make you wrong.

Reflections:

How do I react these days when I'm feeling anxious, angry or judgmental?

What do I do to be restored to sanity?

How did I handle my anxiety before I entered recovery?

Was I in the habit of blaming others?

Do I have an awareness of when I'm in self-centered fear?

How do I get reconnected to my Higher Power?

Week Three

"God can't give you anything new until you let go of the old."

I hate change. For some reason I'm convinced that things will get worse if they change, and even if things aren't so good now I'd rather they stay the same rather than risk a change. I was told when I came into the program that I would only have to change one thing, and I was relieved to hear that. But then they told me that one thing was everything! I quickly realized that the first thing I needed to change was my attitude about change.

A good friend of mine in the program has a different view on change. She says that you can't know what you don't know. "How many times do things get better after they change?" she asks. When I think about this and look at my experience, I find that they almost always get better. "Then why not look at change as a chance for improvement and turn the results over to your Higher Power?" she suggests.

The more I follow my friend's advice, the easier it is for me to handle change. A couple of days ago my wireless router went out and it felt like the end of the world. After I calmed down, it occurred to me that I might get a more powerful router and actually have improved wireless coverage in my home. Now that was a change! These days when things change, I ask myself how they have improved or how I can make them better. Once I put my focus here, I find it's easier to let go and even look forward to change.

What I've learned is that God can't give me anything new until I let go of the old.

Reflections:

How attached am I to having things remain the same?

Do I fear change?

What is my actual experience to things changing versus my fears about change?

Have I ever considered that before God gives me anything better, things have to change first?

Am I willing to change my ideas about change?

Do I ever consider that change might be good?

Week Four

"Getting stuck means you are in between surrenders."

Before recovery, I felt stuck in many areas of my life. I was stuck in a job I hated, stuck in unhealthy relationships I didn't know how to get out of, and stuck in an endless cycle of drinking and using. With no tools to help me, my life continued to spin out of control. Once I reached my bottom, though, I finally surrendered and my recovery began.

When I started the steps, I was introduced to a whole new life. I learned new ways of thinking, new ways of acting, and I also learned new ways to be stuck. Because of my old ideas and my resistance, I soon became stuck on the third step, and it was a long time before I surrendered to God's will. Then I was stuck on the fourth step, and once again it took a while to surrender to the process of an inventory. Oddly, even though the tool of surrender always worked, I usually insisted on being stuck for a while before I would use it.

Today I'm much quicker to recognize when I'm stuck and to do something about it. Today my tolerance for pain is small, and whenever I'm feeling uncomfortable, I immediately ask myself what I'm afraid of or what I'm resisting. As soon as I'm clear on what it is, I surrender and ask for God's will and direction. As always, this restores me to sanity and to the serenity I've come to cherish in my life.

Today I know that when I'm stuck, it just means I'm
in between surrenders.

Reflections:

In what areas of my life did I feel stuck before recovery?

What finally brought me to the surrender of recovery?

Did I become stuck in the beginning?

Am I stuck now?

What do I do when I'm in fear?

How often do I ask for God's will and direction in my life?

Month Two

Week Five

"I've learned to say, 'You may be right.'"

Before recovery, I thought I knew it all. When someone disagreed with me, I'd argue and go out of my way to set them straight. I loved the saying, "Those people who think they know it all are especially annoying to those of us who do," and in the end I was self-righteous and smug. It's no wonder I didn't have many friends left.

When I began working with my sponsor, I started arguing with him, too. At first he listened to me, but after a while he'd had enough. "Why don't you take the cotton out of your ears and put it in your mouth," he suggested. I was too desperate to be indignant, so I followed his advice and began listening to what others were sharing in meetings. And that's when the miracle began for me.

Through listening to the experience, strength and hope of others, I not only learned that my way was not the only way; I learned that it was almost certainly not the right way for you. I learned that others had their own path, made their own mistakes and grew from their own experiences, and I came to see that your opinions were just as valuable as mine.

Most of all I learned to stop arguing because I learned how to say,
"You may be right."

Reflections:

Did I used to think I knew it all before recovery?

How often did I try to get others to see my side of things?

When I came into the program, did I think most people were wrong?

How long did it take before I truly began listening to what others had to say?

Do I finally give others the space and the respect to do what they think is right for them even though I don't agree?

How often do I say, "You may be right" and leave it at that?

Week Six

"Don't forget that the world record is 24 hours."

I remember when I was new watching people take cakes for five years, seven years and more, and thinking that they had something I didn't - the ability to stay sober. When I shared about this, I was told that we all have the same amount of time - today. As I kept going to meetings, I started to see people with long term recovery go out, and learned how important it was to value and concentrate on today.

As I got a few years under my belt and began trying to figure out what to do with my life, I once again got impatient when I saw that others had accomplished so much and seemed to have many of the things that I wanted, too. When I shared this, I was once again reminded that the world record was just 24 hours and that if I set a goal and took the next daily action, then I could also accomplish anything I set my mind to.

Over the years, I've come to see the immense wisdom and simplicity in today's quote. When tasks or goals seem impossible to accomplish or overcome, I remind myself that while I may not be able to keep it up or do it over a lifetime, I can do it just for today.

And what I've found is that when I take the right action, one 24-hour day at a time, obstacles are overcome and dreams do come true.

Reflections:

How did I feel in the beginning when I saw people celebrate long term recovery?

When did I learn the value of appreciating what I had today?

What was my reaction as I saw that other people had the things I wanted?

Did I ever compare my insides with someone else's outsides?

Do I still do that today?

Have I learned that I can truly accomplish anything if I take it one 24 hour day at a time?

Week Seven

"If the grass is greener on the other side, it's because they are putting fertilizer on it!"

I've spent a lot of my life envying what other people had, resenting I didn't have it too, and feeling I deserved it. I've always felt smarter, more talented, better looking, and more suited for the success I've seen others enjoying. I never understood why others seemed to have all the breaks until I entered recovery, and then I got a harsh lesson...

As I started to share my feelings of entitlement with my sponsor, he began to ask me some difficult (for me!) questions. "Why didn't you stay in college?" he asked. "Money is in sales, not college," I answered. "If you think you'd be such a great actor, why haven't you taken acting classes?" "Ah, it's not what you know, it's who you know," I scoffed. After a while, he pointed out that I had all the answers except the one that mattered.

It took me a long time before I could admit that perhaps the reason I wasn't successful was because I wasn't doing the things that successful people do. As childish as it may sound, I learned that the world wasn't waiting to give me things just because of who I thought I was. It took a while, but now I get it:

If the grass is greener on the other side, it's because they are putting fertilizer on it!

Reflections:

How envious was I of others when I entered recovery?

Did I feel I deserved the success I saw others enjoying?

Was I doing much to be successful myself?

How long did it take before I saw that my actions equaled my results?

Do I still feel entitled today?

What am I doing to earn my success today?

Week Eight

"There are some days when I say, "What program?" "God who?"

Last week my business website was hacked, my site was taken down, and my account was suspended. For hours, while I lost revenue and customers, I pleaded, begged and threatened my hosting company's technical support. For the most part I was polite and professional, but I was cursing under my breath, anxious and pissed off. After it was all over, I was a wreck. Later that evening, I wondered why I hadn't brought God into it and why I hadn't worked my program.

What I realized is that fear is still the chief activator of my character defects, and prime among them is fear of losing something I have or of not getting what I demand. As I furiously instant messaged and E-Mailed their support, I saw eight years of work go down the drain, felt the pain of starting over, and grew increasingly resentful. Thankfully everything was resolved in a few hours, but for a while I was alone and spiritually vulnerable.

As I reflect back on the experience, I'm amazed by how quickly I can abandon my program when I'm in fear. I completely understand when I hear of people who pick up a drink after 20 years and can't explain why. I know that alcoholism is cunning, baffling and powerful, and I'm constantly reminded that I must remain vigilant.

Because even after all my time in recovery, there are some days when I say, "What program?" "God who?"

Reflections:

When was the last time I forgot my program?

How do I react when I'm in fear?

Have I ever been close to a relapse?

What did I do to regain my sanity?

What do I think when I hear of others who go out?

How can I make sure that doesn't become me?

Month Three

Week Nine

"I'll never be happy as long as I keep comparing my insides with someone else's outsides."

I don't know about you, but it is very easy for me to feel less than. I'm constantly comparing myself to other people and asking why I don't have a newer car, a bigger house or more money. I'm convinced that most people are happier than I am, know something I don't, or are having a better life. While I've always felt something was wrong with me, it wasn't until I entered recovery that I found out what it was.

I remember having this discussion with my sponsor and him telling me that alcoholism is a disease of perception. He told me there are three beliefs most alcoholics have that will forever prevent them from being happy. First, he said that we believe that what we don't have is almost certainly better than what we do have. Second is that no matter how much we have of something, we're sure that having more of it would be better. And the third belief is that when we finally get what we want, then we'll be happy.

Now, I don't know how he read my mind, but that sure described me! When I asked him what I was supposed to do next, he told me that God could and would restore me to sanity if I was willing to work the steps. I was. It's taken years, but today I have an attitude of gratitude, I'm comfortable in my own skin, and I have a peace and serenity that no car or amount of money could ever give me.

And best of all, I'm truly happy because I no longer feel the need to compare my insides with someone else's outsides.

Reflections:

Have I struggled with feelings of being less than?

How did I used to deal with these feelings?

Do I identify with the "three beliefs" of an alcoholic?

Have I found a solution to that kind of thinking?

Am I comfortable in my own skin today?

If not, what have I found that works to make me feel better about myself?

Week Ten

"It's the first drink that gets you drunk."

For years, this saying made no sense to me. It wasn't the first drink, I argued, but rather the seventh or tenth drink that got me drunk. I'd been able to control my drinking for a long time, and with a lot of willpower, I'd been able to limit my drinking to a few glasses. Toward the end though, I'd inevitably have that sixth or seventh or more drink and end up roaring drunk. If only I could regain control, I thought, and when I entered the program, I secretly hoped I'd learn how.

I remember sharing with my sponsor my desire to once again control and enjoy my drinking. He said, "Heck, when I controlled my drinking, I didn't enjoy it, and when I enjoyed it, I couldn't control it." Boy did that make sense. He then told me that for him, one drink was too much and a thousand was never enough, because once he started, he could no longer stop. And that's when I began to understand.

Today I know very well that if I began drinking again, even one drink, it would soon enough lead to ten, and I'd be drunk. I don't know when I crossed the line into full blown alcoholism, but I did. I now know there is no going back. The good news is that I no longer fantasize about being able to control it again, because I know that it's the first drink that will get me drunk.

Reflections:

How long did I try to control my drinking or using?

When I got sober, did I secretly think I'd be able to regain control?

What happened for me that changed my mind about this?

Does the thought ever occur to me that perhaps in the future I could probably handle it?

Do I think that thought through?

Am I OK with never drinking and using again?

Week Eleven

"The minute I take control, that's when I lose control."

I used to try to control my drinking and using all the time. I'd give myself a limit as to how many drinks I would have; I'd practice drinking a glass of water between cocktails; I would use only on the weekend (that didn't work because soon Friday and then Thursday became part of the weekend), and on and on. What I found was that as soon as I tried to control it, I lost control.

When I entered recovery I learned about the concept of powerlessness. Even though I had countless examples of how I was powerless over drugs and alcohol, I secretly hoped that one day I would be able to control and enjoy it. After countless inventories and step work, I learned that I lost that dubious luxury long ago. Whenever I tried to control my drinking, I didn't enjoy it, and when I enjoyed it, I couldn't control it.

Just as I was coming to accept my powerlessness over alcohol, I faced an even more daunting idea - that I was powerless over just about everything else in my life as well. The way I've come to accept this is to take responsibility for my part (my thoughts and my actions) and to leave the rest up to God. This always works, when I remember to work it.

And the minute I don't, the minute I take control, that's the minute I lose control once again.

Reflections:

What kind of things did I used to try to control my drinking and using?

How did this work?

When I entered recovery, what was my reaction to the idea of powerlessness?

Did I harbor any secret wishes?

Do I accept that I'm powerless over people, places and things today?

When I try to control things, what happens?

Week Twelve

"Things might not get better for me, but I can get better despite things."

When I was a newcomer, I was convinced that because I was now sober, things in my life would get better. I was sure my career would finally get on track, my relationships would improve, etc., and I knew that as those things came together, I would finally be happy. In fact, I secretly felt like I deserved for things to improve now that I was being "good." Boy, was I wrong.

What actually happened was that my life started to spiral out of control. It was as if things had a natural momentum to them, and even though I wasn't acting the same way, the wreckage of my past was beginning to catch up with me. As I grew more and more miserable, my sponsor taught me something that set me free.

I remember he sat me down and asked me if I could make it through the day without a drink or a drug. I told him I could, and that's when he taught me that while I may not be able to control all the things in my life, I could control the most important thing of all - my sobriety and my recovery. He told me that if I took care of that, then all the other "things" would work out.
While at first I didn't believe him, it turns out he was right.

*Today I know that while things may not always get better for me,
I can get better if I focus on the one thing that matters.*

Reflections:

Was I convinced that entering recovery would solve all my problems?

What actually happened?

How did I deal with this?

When did I finally learn the difference between what I can control and what I can't?

How much do I focus on my recovery today?

How are the things in my life today?

Week Thirteen

"God doesn't care what you think about Him, only that you think about Him."

I've spend a lot of my life struggling with the concept of God. For many years my God was on a throne judging my thoughts and actions, and I did my best to keep on His good side. When I sinned, I'd try doubly hard to be good again and all the while I was trying to keep track of my good/bad ledger. "If I die tonight, where will I end up?" I thought regularly before going to sleep. By the time I got sober, I was pretty sure where I was going...

In early recovery I was terrified of the thought of turning my will and my life over to the care of God as I understood Him. I was sure God didn't care much for me, and I was afraid that if I abandoned myself to Him, then he would exact His just reward. I secretly resented God, and when I finally admitted this to my sponsor, he gave me the solution.

"Talk to God and tell Him exactly how you feel," he suggested. "But I'm really pissed off about a lot of things, and He's not going to like it," I warned him. "Believe me, He's big enough to take whatever you've got," he said. When I finally began an open and honest dialogue with God - telling Him of my anger, resentments, fears and disappointments in Him - that's when my connection and faith in a Higher Power began. And that's when my real recovery began as well.

Today I've learned that God doesn't care what you think about Him, only that you think about Him.

Reflections:

What was my early concept of God like?

Did I bring this concept of God into the rooms with me?

How did this affect my surrender to a Higher Power?

Was I afraid of retribution from God when I was a newcomer?

When did I finally begin to talk honestly with God?

What is my connection and faith like today?

Month Four

Week Fourteen

"I may not know how to make it better, but I sure know how to make it worse."

I remember how bad things were before recovery, and how easy it was for me to make them worse. If my job wasn't going well, I'd cop an attitude, show up late, or start slacking off (more than I already was!) If my relationship wasn't going the way I thought it should, I'd shut down and withhold - all with the justified thought, "I'll show her." No matter what was going wrong, I always found a way to make it worse.

When I entered recovery, my sponsor taught me that what happened in my life was my responsibility. He showed me how I had a part in everything that happened to me and how my solutions often became worse than the original problem. It took many years for me to accept this and many more to learn how to make better choices. Thank God I had the twelve steps to teach me how.

I once heard someone say that the program was the life manual they wish they would have had when growing up. I completely relate to this because now I, too, know how to handle situations that used to baffle me. Best of all, though, by staying focused on my part, I know how to make things better.

Today I have a choice between making the situations in my life better or worse, and most of the time I make the right choice.

Reflections:

How did I handle problems before recovery?

Were my solutions sometimes worse than my problems?

Was I used to pointing the finger at others?

What was my reaction to the idea that what happened in my life was my responsibility?

How long did it take for me to fully accept this as true?

Do I now know how to make the situations in my life better? If so, how do I do this?

Week Fifteen

"The longer I'm sober, the drunker I was."

Denial is an amazing thing. When I first entered the program, I had no intention of staying sober longer than a few months; I just needed to pull things together a little, get myself under control again. I wasn't like the real alcoholics I heard share in meetings, and I was sure I could control my drinking again once I cooled it a bit. After all, it hadn't been that bad, I told myself.

As the fog cleared, though, and I began journaling and working the steps, more began to be revealed to me. I especially remember sitting in meetings listening to people share about being arrested for drunk driving and thinking that never happened to me. I was sober over a year before I remembered that when I was seventeen I crashed my car into two parked cars and was arrested for reckless drunk driving. That was a humbling memory...

As I peel back the layers of my past and uncover the truth about my drinking and using history, I'm amazed at how lucky I've been. I've heard that prisons are packed with alcoholics and addicts who never found sobriety, and I now know I could easily have been one of them.

Today my denial is gone and the longer I stay sober, the drunker I realize I was.

Reflections:

Was I in denial about how bad it was when I was a newcomer?

Did I think I could resume drinking or using after I got things together a little?

When did I realize that I was an alcoholic?

What do I think about my drinking and using history today?

How grateful am I that I'm sober today?

What am I doing to stay that way?

Week Sixteen

"Live life today as though you knew you were dying."

We've all heard sayings like this before, and for many years my reaction was, "Yeah, but it's not my last day and the rent is due at the end of the month, and my relationship isn't getting better, and blah, blah, blah." As the many worries of the future consumed me, the precious days and years passed by without me, and now, at 13 years of sobriety, I wonder where the time went.

I remember when I got 30 days, an old timer with 24 years shook my hand and congratulated me. I said, "Gee, I wish I had 24 years," and I'll never forget what he said. "I'll trade you my 24 years, right now, for your 30 days!" It took me many years to see the wisdom in this: It's about the journey, not the destination.

These days, I'm very aware of the gift of another day alive and sober. I've seen a lot of people go out or even die, and today I live from a place of supreme gratitude. Life is precious, beautiful and filled with opportunities to help people and make a real difference. I appreciate my life today, and I'm grateful that I'm present enough to enjoy it.

Today I live life as though I were dying, and I'm fully alive because of it.

Reflections:

What do I think when I hear sayings like this?

Do I live in the present much, or am I consumed with worries of the future?

Was I in a rush to get time in the program?

When I look back on my early days, would I have done things differently?

What would I have done?

Do I enjoy my life today?

Week Seventeen

"It's progress, not perfection. We are not saints."

I had some friends over the other night for dinner and we started talking about road rage. We each had a story to tell about how we had participated in an escalating episode of honking, cutting off, or giving the finger to another angry driver. Being generally centered in other areas of my life, I was a little disappointed in myself when I realized that I, too, can become a complete asshole in about 15 seconds.

When I entered the program, I was used to acting this way. In general, I had a low regard for other people's feeling, and one of the problems I had with the steps was that I thought if I didn't become a saint, I wouldn't get sober. I remember telling my sponsor this and him saying four words that I still repeat to this day: "It's progress, not perfection."

I've made A LOT of progress over the years, and I've come a long way from where I've been. For the most part, I'm comfortable in my own skin, I'm truly grateful for what I have, and I sincerely try to add to people's lives. And yet every now and then, sometimes without my even being aware of it, something will provoke me into a state of fear and I'll resort temporarily to an old behavior. Thankfully, I'm able to recover my serenity pretty quickly, and when I do I remind myself:

"It's progress, not perfection. We are not saints."

Reflections:

How do I react to road rage these days?

Where do I think my reaction comes from?

How did I treat people before recovery?

Am I an "all or nothing" thinker?

How would I rate my overall happiness today?

Do I remember that it's progress, not perfection?

Month Five

Week Eighteen

"When you own your part, you own your power."

When I was new to the program, I dreaded doing my fourth step inventory. What possible good could it do me to list all my resentments, I wondered. When my sponsor told me there was an invisible category called "my part," I was sure this was going to be a useless exercise. I mean, I didn't have a part in choosing my parents, or my siblings, or what happened to me at school and on and on. Just thinking about it made me resentful!

After months of painful and exhaustive writing, I finally finished the first draft of my inventory. I remember reading it to my sponsor and becoming more and more irritated each time he asked me about my part. "But I'm talking about what he, she, or it did to me," I complained. "Yes, but yours is the only part you can change," he said. And that's when I began to understand.

I had spent a lifetime blaming other people, places and things for the misery in my life, and all that did was make me a perpetual victim. Once I learned to focus on my part, however, I began to see the role my own behavior played in the destructive patterns in my life. And that's when I discovered I had the power to change them.

You see, I learned that when you own your part, you own your power.

Reflections:

How did I feel about the fourth step when I first heard about it?

What did I think about the column of "my part?"

What was my experience like in doing my fourth step?

How did my fifth step go?

At what point did I stop blaming other people for the misery in my life?

Have I completely owned my part today?

Week Nineteen

"Develop an 'Attitude of Gratitude.'"

I have a secret weapon in my recovery tool bag: the Gratitude List. Oh I know, you've heard all about gratitude lists, but when was the last time you made one? Whenever I'm feeling overwhelmed, stressed or in fear, the fastest way out is for me to make a quick list of 50 things I'm grateful for.

When I mention this to people, their first reaction is "50?!" If 50 seems like a lot to you, too, it's just because you're not in the habit of making gratitude lists. The secret is to list the things you're grateful for that are centered on what you are feeling anxious or fearful about.

For example, when I'm in financial fear, I list all the things around finances I'm grateful for. These usually include that today I have a place to sleep; my rent is paid; the electricity is working (and it helps when I think of all the people who don't even have electricity!); I have money in my pocket; I've always earned money and did so yesterday or last week/month, etc. This works for every topic, and after you get started, 50 comes easy.

Today my life is good; I'm appreciative and I know serenity because I know how to develop and live in an attitude of gratitude.

Reflections:

When was the last time I made a gratitude list?

How many items were on it?

Is it easy or hard for me to list 50 things I'm grateful for?

Have I ever made specific gratitude lists?

How do I feel after I've made a Gratitude list?

Why don't I do them more often?

Week Twenty

"If I don't go to meetings, I don't hear what God wants me to hear."

Before recovery, I kept a lot of lower companion company. I worked with a bunch of self-serving thieves who wanted the easy way out at the expense of others. My friends were alcoholics or drug addicts who were great to party with, but not much help when I needed to move. Eventually I ended up lower than them all, and was isolated, angry and out of options.

When I crawled into the rooms, it was suggested that I go to a lot of meetings and start paying attention to what I heard. When one of my old friends said that I was being brainwashed, I brought this up to my sponsor. He told me that from what he had heard from me so far, my brain could use some washing! As much as I didn't want to admit it, he was right, and over the years I've heard exactly what I've needed to hear from someone sharing in a meeting.

I've always been in awe of the wisdom that comes from the rooms. Even today, when I think I know it all, I'm amazed by what can come out of a newcomer's mouth. When I'm feeling scared, discouraged, or disconnected, I almost always hear just what I need to change my perspective and find a solution. Today, when I'm feeling too busy or too comfortable to go, I remind myself that if I don't keep going to meetings, I won't keep hearing what God wants me to hear.

Reflections:

What were my friends like before recovery?

Did I think I was better than they were?

What did I think of the things I heard in the rooms in the beginning?

How long did it take for me to see the wisdom of the rooms?

Are there times when I just don't feel like going to another meeting?

What is my experience like when I take contrary action and go anyway?

Week Twenty-one

"Anything an alcoholic lets go of has claw marks all over it."

Before recovery, I tried to control everything. I would lie in bed at night planning my days and weeks, and I would make endless lists of activities I could follow that would lead to specific results. I played and replayed conversations that were sure to take place to make sure they came out the way I wanted them to. When the last thing I tried to control - my alcohol use - spun out of control, I finally surrendered.

When I got sober, I had to let go of all my plans and schemes for controlling my drinking and drug use. Because I was at bottom, it was easy for me to abandon my old ideas and to ask God to restore me to sanity. Just because this worked for my alcoholism, though, didn't mean I was willing to turn the rest of my life over. "God, you can have my drinking, but I'll handle the rest," was my attitude. You can imagine how that went for me.

What I've learned over the years is that my life gets better in direct proportion to my willingness to trust God with the other areas of it. It continues to be hard to let go and act with faith - especially when I'm in fear - but each time I do, I'm rewarded with a freedom and a joy that could never have come so long as I continued to try to control things. Today, if I'm not willing to let go, then I pray for the willingness to be willing.

And once I withdraw my claws, God takes over and the healing begins.

Reflections:

How controlling was I before I entered recovery?

What were some of the ways I would scheme to get my way?

How did this usually work out for me?

Was it hard to let go and let God in the beginning?

What did it take for me to finally turn these areas over?

What do I still have my claws buried in today?

Month Six

Week Twenty-two

"The only thing worse than my problems are my solutions to them."

Before recovery, I couldn't understand why my life wasn't getting better despite what I did to fix it. If my boss was a jerk, I'd quit. If my girlfriend wasn't paying attention to me, I'd go out with someone else. If my landlord didn't like it when I was late with the rent, I'd move. No matter what I tried, things only seemed to get worse.

When I began working the program, I told my sponsor all about my problems. He listened for a while and then asked me how good of an employee, boyfriend, and renter I had been. At first I was insulted, but then he told me to carefully write about each problem focusing only on my part. Well, that certainly opened my eyes.

After many thorough inventories, what I've found is that all my problems start with me, and the reason my solutions make them worse is because they are driven by the same selfishness or self-centered fear that caused them to begin with. Today, the only solutions that work start by acknowledging where I've been at fault, and end with a sincere desire and offer to make amends.

Today I have solutions that make my life better.

Reflections:

What was my life like before recovery?

Were my solutions making my life better or worse?

What was my reaction to my first inventory?

How long did it take me to see all of my part?

Am I in the habit of doing thorough inventories these days?

How am I at acknowledging my part and offering to make amends?

Week Twenty-three

"My definition of balance is being able to obsess equally in all areas of my life!"

As an alcoholic, I completely understand all or nothing thinking. When I was in my disease, I used to obsessively plan out my drinking and using, always making sure I had the right amount of drugs on me, and I would even drink before meeting friends at the bar just so I could pretend to drink like them. In the end, my obsession consumed me and drove me into the rooms.

Once I started working the steps, I began obsessing on other things. For a while, I was consumed with dying, sure I had done irreparable damage to myself during my years of using. Next, I became obsessed with the fear of financial insecurity, this time convinced I had ruined my professional future. And then I got into a relationship and that obsession nearly drove me to drink. During my sixth step, I realized that I had to surrender my obsessive thinking if I wanted to stay sober.

For me, surrendering my obsessive thinking came down to a question of faith - did I or didn't I trust that my Higher Power would take care of me? As I began to obsess on that, my sponsor told me that faith wasn't a thought but rather an action. He suggested I begin letting go and letting God, and each time I did, my life got a little better.

Today I know that obsessing isn't the answer, turning it over is.

Reflections:

What is my experience with all or nothing thinking?

Do I tend to obsess on things?

When I entered the program, what kinds of things did I obsess on?

How unmanageable is my life when I indulge in obsessive-thinking?

Do I have faith that my Higher Power will take care of me?

How often do I turn my will and my life over these days?

Week Twenty-four

"I wanted to be famous but God made me anonymous."

I had some pretty big plans when I entered the program. Even though my sponsor told me it wasn't about money, property and prestige, I knew better. I was convinced that, being sober, I would finally write the books and create the products that would get me the recognition and riches I deserved. I even told my sponsor how good of a circuit speaker I would be and asked what I needed to do that. He smiled and suggested that a year of sobriety might be a good start.

As I began working the program, I made some startling revelations. In doing inventories, I found that there was a time when I had a lot of money, property and prestige, but I was still miserable. As I did more work, I discovered that the hole I felt inside could never be filled up with anything outside me, and the more I chased that, the emptier I felt. It was only when I surrendered the character defect of feeling terminally unique that I began to feel better.

One of the truest things I've learned in the program is that I will always feel less than when I compare my insides with someone else's outsides. It has taken years, but I now understand why character building and my spiritual connection must come before any outside success if I'm to be happy. And I now appreciate the powerful role anonymity has played in helping me develop these essential qualities.

Today I understand the folly of wanting to be famous, and the wisdom of God's anonymity.

Reflections:

Did I come into the program with some Big Plans?

Was I convinced that money, property and prestige would cure most of my problems?

What did I find out about the hole I felt as I did the work?

How long did I continue to pursue outside things in my attempt to fill this hole?

Do I still compare how I'm feeling on the inside with someone else's outsides?

How has my anonymity helped me to remain right-sized?

Week Twenty-five

"Honesty got me sober; tolerance keeps me sober."

I didn't realize how dishonest I was before I entered recovery. I had half-truths and misleading-by-omission down to a fine art, and by the end of my drinking and using, I was even good at deceiving myself. I didn't know it then, but the practice of being rigorously honest was the cornerstone of my recovery, and without it, I never would have gotten sober.

Another thing I didn't realize before recovery was how intolerant I was of other people, places and things. Once I began looking at myself, I found that my first reactions were to judge, reject and condemn others. What I discovered was that my intolerance was a defense mechanism covering my deep feelings of inferiority and shame, and it wasn't until I discarded these that I began to live comfortably in my own skin.

What I've learned over the years is that if I want to remain comfortable and sober, I've got to continue to practice tolerance. Now when I feel like judging or condemning others, I quickly look within and ask if I'm scared or if I'm feeling less than. Once I'm honest with myself, I'm able to deal with these feelings, and this always restores me to tolerance of myself and others.

Today I realize that honesty got me sober, but that tolerance keeps me that way.

Reflections:

Was I dishonest before recovery?

How important was being rigorously honest when I entered the program?

Do I see how my intolerance of others is almost always a reflection of how I'm feeling about myself?

How often do I do a tenth step when I'm feeling intolerant?

What are the things I do today to feel comfortable in my own skin?

How tolerant of myself and others am I today?

Week Twenty-six

"It all works out in the end. If it hasn't worked out yet, it's not the end."

This is one of the truest quotes I've heard yet. I can't tell you how many times I've stressed and worried about something I was sure wasn't going to work out, only to eventually realize that in the end it all worked out just fine. Sometimes it took months, other times years, but of all the things I've obsessed about, nearly all of them worked out in the end. The key is waiting for the end.

Before recovery, I was more focused on the middle than the end. I was addicted to drama and was sure that all the negative things in my life would only get worse. I secretly liked being a victim and when something started to work out, I quickly pointed to other awful things that were, or could be, happening. As you might imagine, my life never got any better.

When I entered the program, I was sure that it, too, wouldn't work out. I spent many months trying to convince anyone who would listen why my life would end in disaster. Their answer was always the same: Keep coming back. What I eventually learned was that with the right thought and actions, and with a faith in a Higher Power, things did work out in the end.

And I learned that if it hasn't worked out yet, then it's not the end.

Reflections:

How many times have I stressed and worried about something not working out?

What ended up happening?

Can I remember what I was so worried about a year or two ago?

How much do I focus on taking the next right step and thinking right thoughts?

Am I in the practice of praying and asking God for the right thought, action or inspiration?

How does my life go when I do this?

Month Seven

Week Twenty-seven

"Our neighbor's window looks much cleaner if we first wash our own."

Now that it's hot again, I've begun sleeping with the windows open to let some of the cooler evening air in. My neighbor must have the same idea because her window is open as well, and the sound of her TV carries in the still summer air, making it hard to go to sleep sometimes. Even though she's 82 years old and probably hard of hearing and is the perfect neighbor otherwise, I easily become indignant and start with the, "How dare she!" ranting. How soon I tend to forget...

For years while drinking and using, I carried on like a madman. I played my music as loud as I could stand, late into the night, and often partied with friends and family on the patio next to my neighbor's living room. I had no awareness or concern for anyone but myself, and through it all, my neighbor remained calm and respectful and never said a word. You'd think that now that I'm in recovery, I'd have more empathy and understanding, but that's not always my first reaction.

What I've found is that I have little initial tolerance for behaviors I used to practice with abandon. As an ex-smoker, for example, I'm an anti-smoker now and am irritated and resentful if someone smokes within 20 feet of me. Through it all, I have learned to continually ask for understanding and tolerance from my Higher Power, and I've learned that it's up to me to take the high road and set the example with my behavior. And I find that when I do, everything works out for the best.

I find that my neighbor's window looks much cleaner when I wash my own first.

Reflections:

Before recovery, how might my behavior have offended others?

Was I aware of it at the time?

How do I react when other people engage in the behaviors I used to practice?

How tolerant am I?

Am I quick to ask my Higher Power for the right thought or action?

When I wash my window first, how does doing so affect my view of my neighbor?

Week Twenty-eight

"It's a simple program for complicated people."

They say that this is a simple program, but that it's very hard to follow. I heard this in the beginning of my recovery, but when I read the steps I didn't see why. In fact, the program seemed simple, and I confidently told my sponsor that I could get through the steps in a couple of months. I can still see his smile as he told me, "Let's take it one day at a time." When I finally started, I saw what he meant.

"How can such a simple program be so hard to work?" I quickly began asking myself. What I found was that each step asked me to do something I had never done before - and that was to uncover my beliefs, discover how I had twisted them to serve my own selfish ends, and then discard them for God's will rather than my own. Simple, yes, but not easy to do!

Over the years, I've found that this program is much easier to work if/when I quit making it so complicated. And the way I do that is by still trying to force my will on things. I now know it's much simpler when I evaluate my motives, seek truly to be of service, and ask for God's will, not mine, to be done. This truly is the easier, softer way.

Today I understand when they say that this is a simple program for complicated people!

Reflections:

When was the first time I heard today's quote?

What was my response to it?

How do I make this simple program complicated?

Do I still try to force my will onto people, places and things?

How does that turn out for me and others?

Have I yet found the easier, softer way?

Week Twenty-nine

"You're exactly where you're supposed to be."

For as long as I can remember, I've been unhappy where I was and wished I was somewhere else. In school I always wanted to be in the next grade; at work I wanted a more senior position making more money; when I bought my first home, I quickly wanted one with a pool. When I entered recovery, I brought this same impatience and unhappiness into the rooms with me.

I remember complaining to my sponsor after a few months that things hadn't gotten better, and that I even felt worse. He listened patiently and then said, "You're exactly where you're supposed to be." This didn't make sense to me, and as my life continued to unravel and as I grew more frustrated, irritated and angry, I kept complaining. His answer remained the same, and it took years before I finally understood what he meant.

One of the most important things I've learned in recovery is that accepting where I am physically, emotionally and spiritually is the necessary key to changing it. Once I stop resenting how things are or wishing they were different, I can begin working with God to make them better. But it all begins with acceptance of where I am right now.

Today I know that I'm exactly where I should be, and I know how to make it better.

Reflections:

How often do I wish my life was different?

Has it ever changed into what I thought I wanted?

What did I feel like then?

How good am I at accepting things as they are?

Once I'm in acceptance, how do things change for me?

Do I accept that I'm right where I'm supposed to be right now?

Week Thirty

"When you get to your wit's end, you'll find that God lives there."

Before recovery, when I got to the bottom, I just moved over and started digging another hole. I would leave jobs, relationships, and even states looking for a different solution. I didn't have a God in my life, so there was no turning it over. It wasn't until I had broken my shovel and hit my final bottom that I was ready to admit complete defeat.

When I came into the rooms, I heard a lot about God. I didn't like it. I had given up on Him a long time ago, and I was sure He had deserted me. What I came to find out was that God was always there to help me when I hit bottom. What I also learned, years later, was that He was there for me all along - I just had to ask for help sooner.

What I now know is that I don't have to wait until I'm at my wit's end to reach out and get help from God. He lives in me and is with me every step of the way. The key that opens the lock is and always has been willingness. And today, I'm much more willing to be willing.

Today, I know I don't have to reach my wit's end to find out where God lives.

Reflections:

How many bottoms did I dig before recovery?

What did I do when I hit one?

How far did I have to go before I finally turned to God?

When did I become willing to reach out to God sooner?

Do I still have a high tolerance for pain?

What can I do to change this?

Month Eight

Week Thirty-one

"Everyone wants to feel better, but no one wants to change."

Before recovery, I did a lot of things to feel better. I moved, changed jobs, girlfriends, cars, tried different combinations of drugs and alcohol, took up yoga, joined a gym - the list is endless. While these things worked briefly, inevitably I would be left feeling that giant hole inside of me, a hole that always made me miserable.

When I entered recovery, I had the same initial relief as when I tried other new ways to distract myself. After a while though, it, too, began to wear off and I could sense the hole returning. I met with my sponsor, and he told me I was feeling this way because I was resisting and refusing to change. "But I'm sober!" I told him. "Yeah, but you're still trying to do things your way. Until you surrender and really work the steps, you'll just be the same old you – only you'll be miserable and sober this time."

Thank God my sponsor was willing to tell me the truth, and thank God I was ready to hear it. Deep down, I knew I was the common denominator in all the things I had tried that didn't work, and once I got to step four and honestly looked at my part in things, I finally realized what had to change: Me. While thoroughly working the steps, the promises began to come true for me, and today I am not the same man who entered the rooms all those years ago. Today I am happy, joyous and free.

And that is worth changing for.

Reflections:

What were some of the things I used to feel better before recovery?

How did they work for me?

When I entered the program, did I suddenly expect to feel better?

Did I try to do the program my way at first?

When did I finally surrender?

Have I changed in recovery, and, if so, how?

Week Thirty-two

"It is the mosquitoes that will chase me out of the woods, not the bears!"

It's amazing how I intuitively know how to handle the big things. A few weeks ago my brother and his wife - who live right around the corner from me - came home from vacation to find their home had been robbed. At 2 a.m. they were pounding on my door, waking me up from a dead sleep. I sprang into action getting them online, calming them down, and helping in any way I could. If only I could handle the little things as easily...

Last week I noticed my kitchen faucet had come loose from the sink. Each time I turn it on, it wiggles back and forth, and I can't decide what to do about it. I looked underneath and there doesn't seem to be any way to tighten it, and I don't want to spend $200 on a plumber to fix it. I'm beginning to obsess on it and now that it's started to drip a bit, I'm at my wits end!

Even though the little things can still paralyze me and leave me feeling helpless, thank God I have a program that has taught me what to do. I've learned to reach out to others and find someone who has experience with what I'm going through. I now know that I don't have to fix everything at once, rather, I just have to take the next indicated action. And most of all, I've learned how to ask for help.

Today, with the guidance of the program, I know how to handle both the big AND the little things.

Reflections:

How am I at handling the big things?

Before recovery, did the little things ever make me feel over-whelmed?

What tools have I developed to handle the little things today?

Do I remember that I only need to take the next indicated action?

How often do I reach out for help?

How do I feel when I'm of help to others?

Week Thirty-three

"We didn't get here because we sang too loud in church."

It's amazing how self-righteous we alcoholics can sometimes be. Before recovery, many of us acted in destructive, demoralizing and often illegal ways, many times hurting ourselves and others in the process. Rather than being remorseful when confronted with our behaviors, we usually became resentful and acted even more inappropriately. In the end, many of us were alone, and the only people who were glad to see us were the people who welcomed us into recovery.

At first it's hard to confront the damage we've done, but after a while many of us do recover the positions and self-respect we had lost. What also returns, though, is our ego, and sometimes a new sense of entitlement can make us hard to be around again. I have sat and seethed in meetings while people shared how they thought things should be run, all the while harboring my own self-righteous views.

My favorite saying of Bill W's is, "Honesty got me sober and tolerance keeps me that way." When I catch myself feeling mightier than thou, I ask God to remind me of this, and to remind me where I came from. When I do, I'm humbled by the miracle that has taken place in my life, and once again I become right-sized.

I am instantly reminded that we didn't get here because we sang too loud in church.

Reflections:

How much damage did I do before recovery?

What was my reaction to people who called me out on my behavior?

How long did it take for me to get my self-respect back?

In what ways do I act self-righteously today?

How do I get right-sized again?

Do I practice tolerance today?

Week Thirty-four

"It's OK to look back, just don't stare."

A few weeks ago my brother published a memoir about the early years of our family's life in this country (we emigrated from England in the late 50's). It tells the story of the rapid and painful break-up of our family due to my father's alcoholism, and there are some harrowing scenes that were painful for me to read. When I finished the book, I was pretty shaken up, but after a few days I felt myself again. I was grateful for this and remembered that it wasn't always this way.

Before recovery, I was lost in the resentment, fear and misunderstanding of my upbringing. I spent many years secretly wishing it had been different, and many more hating what had happened and what had been done to me. When I looked back on it, I would dwell on the wrongs that had been done, and the loathing I had for "them" soon turned into the self-loathing of my own alcoholism. Without recovery, it surely would have destroyed me as it had my family.

Through recovery, I have learned to sift through my past to find the lessons and even the gifts it has to offer. I know now that my upbringing and my experiences allow me to help others in a way that no one else can. This is one of the miracles of recovery. Today I don't have to relive my past, but I don't have to shut the door on it either.

Today I know that it's OK to look back, as long as I don't stare.

Reflections:

How did I used to feel about my upbringing before recovery?

Did I used to dwell on the wrongs that had been done to me?

How did my resentments affect my life?

What is my experience with self-loathing?

At what point did I come to see my experiences as useful to me and others?

How do I feel about my past today?

Month Nine

Week Thirty-five

"Today is the tomorrow you worried about yesterday, so live in the now."

When I came into the program, I was so consumed with worry for my future that I couldn't even talk about what I was doing in the present. "But what happens if I lose my house; how about my career? What if I go to jail?" These and other future events were my new obsession once I put the drugs and alcohol down.

When I tried to tell others in the program my concerns, they gave me suggestions that seemed ludicrous at the time. "Help stack the chairs after the meeting," they told me. "Collect the coffee cups and go into the kitchen and help the others clean up," they advised. "Aren't you listening?" I wanted to scream at them. Instead, I washed cups...

It has taken years for me to finally learn the lessons they were trying to teach me, but it's clear now. Today, I have everything I need to be happy, joyous and free. And if I take care of the things in front of me today, then one day at a time my life can and will improve.

I now know that today is the tomorrow I worried about yesterday,
so I now make the most out of living today.

Reflections:

How consumed with the future was I when I was new to the program?

What kind of advice did I get and how did I feel about it?

Did I get any relief from being of service to others in the beginning?

How long did it take for me to begin living in the now?

What do I do today when I find myself consumed with worry for the future again?

Do I make the most out of living my life today?

Week Thirty-six

"For every nut in the program, there is a bolt."

When I first entered the rooms of recovery, I was a little taken aback by some of the strange characters I heard share. Some had been to prison; some had lived on the streets; some had been prostitutes; some were ex-gangsters, and some were still pretty crazy. "These people have nothing in common with me," I told my sponsor. "How are they going to help me get sober?"

"Some of these people may not be able to help you directly," he said. "But the fact that they can get this thing and stay sober shows that you can, too." I saw his point. "Besides that," he continued, "even if they don't have the exact experience you've had, there will be someone else who will. No matter what's going on with you, there will always be somebody who has the experience, strength and hope you'll need."

Over the years, I've found this to be so true. One of the things I've learned to count on is that there always is someone who can help me regardless of what I've been or am going through. This has taught me the value of everyone in the program - not just those that I can identify with.

Now I know that there is a bolt for every nut in the program - even me!

Reflections:

Did I identify with everyone I met when I was a newcomer?

What did I think about those who had stories that were very different from my own?

Did I ever think that if they could recover then perhaps there was a chance for me, too?

When did I realize that no matter what I'm going through, there is always someone who can help me?

Do I see how other people can help those that I can't?

What is my opinion today about others who are different from me?

Week Thirty-seven

"We must learn from the mistakes of others because we won't live long enough to make them all ourselves."

Before recovery, I was very judgmental. I especially liked pointing out other people's mistakes and making fun of how stupid they could be. When I made a mistake, I was quick to blame circumstances or others, and rarely did I take responsibility or admit that perhaps I was to blame. After years of avoiding or evading the consequences of my mistakes, they finally caught up with me and I had to surrender.

When I entered recovery, I was still in denial about my behavior, and each time I heard someone share I would think, "I wasn't that bad," and "They sure need to be here." My sponsor reminded me to listen for the similarities, not the differences, and soon I began to identify not with their actions, but with their feelings. Once I identified with their feelings, I learned the powerful word "yet." I hadn't made those mistakes yet, but if I had continued drinking and using, I probably would have.

Over the years, I've learned to listen to and benefit from other people's experience. Now when I hear of the mistakes others have made, I'm quick to see how I've done something similar, or how I could have easily made the same mistake given similar circumstances. Today I'm grateful for the mistakes I've made and for what they have taught me, and I'm even more grateful for the mistakes of others. You see, I understand that:

> *We must learn from the mistakes of others because we won't live long enough to make them all ourselves.*

Reflections:

How judgmental was I before recovery?

Did I take responsibility for the mistakes I made?

What did I think of others when they shared at meetings?

When did I learn the power of the word "yet"?

Have I finally learned to identify with others?

Am I finally grateful for my mistakes?

Week Thirty-eight

"Negativity is my disease asking me to come out to play."

Before recovery, I had just one voice in my head. Sometimes it was encouraging, even optimistic, but most of the time it was negative and defeatist. It told me things weren't going to get better, so why try? It said things were bad so why not at least feel better by drinking and using? Toward the end, the good part of that voice went away and all I heard was how bad things were and how much worse they were going to get. It's no wonder I hit bottom.

When I entered the program, I heard a lot of talk about the disease of alcoholism. At first my voice told me that was a bunch of crap, and that I was just bad, weak-willed or a loser. But as I got better and the positive voice returned, I discovered it was separate from the negative one. I realized there were actually two voices inside me and I began to understand the disease of alcoholism.

It's taken a long time to nurture and grow the positive voice of recovery, but now I recognize it as the truth spoken to me by my Higher Power. The negative voice is still there sometimes and it surprises me when I hear it, but I know it's my alcoholism, and I've learned to thank it for sharing and then to ignore it.

Today I know that negativity is just my disease asking me to come out to play, and I know now not to listen.

Reflections:

How much of my thinking was negative when I was bottoming out?

What was my opinion of myself then?

Did I believe that alcoholism was a disease?

When did I discover that alcoholism had its own voice?

How do I grow and strengthen the voice of recovery in me?

When the disease of alcoholism speaks to me, what do I say to it?

Week Thirty-nine

"God's message to me is 'Stay out of the way, but be ready!'"

This quote made no sense to me for many years. I mean, in the beginning the whole concept of "turn it over" and "surrender" was as foreign to me as speaking another language. I fought every step of the way to control every aspect of my life and was sure I could do it, too. As I worked the steps, though, I was confronted with the unmanageability and wreckage of my life, and I finally admitted that perhaps I didn't have all the answers.

As I began to surrender to the program, I felt like I was getting a lot of mixed messages. On the one hand I was told to "Let go and let God," yet then I was told to "Suit up and show up." Which is it? I wondered. When do I need to use my will versus when do I turn it all over? This was all very confusing to me for a long time.

Over the years I've finally learned the difference. Today I know that it's my job to prepare to take the next indicated action to the best of my ability and to remain willing. The results, the actions and reactions of others, and many other things, however, are all in God's hands. Today I understand God's message to me is "Stay out of the way, but be ready."

And by continuing to work the program one day at a time, I am.

Reflections:

How did I feel about the surrender portion of the program when I was new?

Did I still try to control my life?

When did I finally become willing to surrender?

Was I ever confused by some of the seemingly conflicting messages I heard?

How long did it take for me to stay focused on the next indicated action?

What does today's quote mean to me?

Month Ten

Week Forty

"I don't have to like the situation, but it's important that I like myself in it."

When I first got sober, I took a job in Beverly Hills as an investment broker selling municipal bonds. I hated getting up at 4:45 in the morning to drive to work, hated making cold calls all day, and hated making just enough to get by. What I hated most, though, was myself. Selling bonds wasn't who I was, but it was all I knew to do at the time, and because my identity was tied to what I did, if I hated that, I hated myself. Because of this, I spent many dark days in the abyss of self-pity and self-loathing.

When I look back on it, I'm surprised I didn't just go back out. Thankfully, the bottom I hit was worse than my day job, and so each night I dragged myself to a meeting to try to find a better way. My sponsor listened patiently as I wallowed in my misery and finally said, "Michael, your job isn't about you or who you are. It's simply a vehicle for you to be of service and to help others. And until you see all of life like that, you will never be happy no matter what you are doing."

It took me years of working the steps and working with others before I saw the wisdom in what he said. Today I understand the importance of being of service, and I find that I like myself a lot more when I'm trying to give rather than get. Because of this I'm able to separate myself from what I have and what I'm doing, and in this way I've learned to live comfortably in my own skin.

Today I may not like all the situations in my life, but I've learned to like myself in them.

Reflections:

How much was my self-worth tied up with what I did when I was new?

How much time did I spend in the abyss of self-pity or self-loathing?

When did I learn about the importance of being of service?

What has my experience been like when I put myself out there for others?

How often am I looking for a way to be of service rather than looking at what's in it for me?

Do I like myself these days?

Week Forty-one

"Before you do something stupid, wait 24 hours..."

Restraint of pen and tongue was a foreign concept to me before I entered the program. Instead, I was impetuous and acted on feelings of jealousy, fear, anger or hurt pride. Fueled by resentment, it was easy for me to justify my actions and ignore the repercussions and reactions of others. When I got into the rooms, I was at odds with most people and alienated even from myself. My life had become unmanageable.

When I began working the steps, I learned to take the focus off what other people were doing to me and look at my own behavior instead. It was hard at first not to stop reacting to the many perceived wrongs I felt people were doing to me, but when I finally learned to put a space between what I felt and how I reacted, my life began to dramatically improve.

Today I've come to rely on the wisdom and the miracles that can happen in between my thoughts and my actions. Time after time, situations will automatically clear themselves up if I only wait, pray on them and turn them over. I am much less likely to become excited or agitated, and I'm much less likely to make things worse if I can just pause before I react.

Today I've learned that before I do something stupid, I should wait at least 24 hours.

Reflections:

How impetuous was I before I entered recovery?

How did my reactions hurt or harm other people or even me?

Was it hard to take the focus off other people and put it on myself?

What were some of the things I learned to do to put a space in between my thoughts and reactions?

If I'm good at doing that now, how do things usually turn out?

Have I finally learned to wait at least 24 hours before I do something stupid?

Week Forty-two

"Bring the body, the mind will follow."

This is a quote I heard early on in my recovery, and it has served me well over the years. Over and over again, when I haven't wanted to go to a meeting, I went anyway and once my body was there, my mind ended up being glad it went along, too. Like much of the wisdom in the program, I can apply the truth in this quote to many other areas of my life as well.

What I've learned is that taking action is almost always the gateway into feeling better. Rarely have I been able to think my way into different behavior or results. Instead, it's only when I take action (especially when I don't want to) that things begin to shift, and I begin feeling better.

The program, like life, doesn't work when I'm into thinking, only when I'm into action.

It's interesting how, even with this knowledge and experience, my mind still tells me not to do the things that will make me feel better. Often I'd rather watch TV than go to a meeting, rest after work than go to the gym, procrastinate rather than take action. The good news, though, is that it always works out for the best when I go ahead and take action anyway.

Whenever I bring my body, my mind always follows...

Reflections:

What experience do I have with "Bring the body, the mind will follow?"

Have I been able to think my way into feeling better?

How often do I still try to?

What are some of the ways I support myself in taking action?

How do I feel when I do?

What actions should I be taking today, and what I can I do to take them?

Week Forty-three

"Drinking gave me the feeling of a job well done without having done a thing."

I remember a restaurant/bar in the rich neighborhood of Brentwood, California I used to go to after work. I'd saddle up to the long, swank bar and order cocktails while I watched the successful people with money come in to have $200 dinners. I was struggling financially at the time and in the beginning I felt out of place, but after a few drinks I had goal-planned my first million and was soon feeling as if I belonged.

Years later in recovery while working on my eighth step making a list of all the people we had harmed and become willing to make amends, I was surprised when my sponsor told me to put my name on it. When I asked why, he told me to list all the things I had wanted to do and what I had wanted to make out of my life, and then write about how alcohol and drugs had taken them away. I thought about that bar in Brentwood and hundreds more like it and of all the plans and goals I had drank and used away.

When they say that alcohol is cunning, baffling and powerful, they mean it in so many insidious ways. When I think of the potential, the future, the life I drank away, I'm sorry to my core. It's hard to forgive myself sometimes. But when I think of all I have accomplished since I got sober, and of the lifetime of dreams still ahead I'm filled with hope and gratitude.

Today I live in and appreciate the miracle of my recovery.

Reflections:

Was I a list-maker and a goal-planner when I was drinking and using?

How did I feel after I had made all my plans?

How many of them did I get around to accomplishing?

When I got sober, did I ever regret all of the time, the life and the dreams I had drank or used away?

Did I forgive myself?

What dreams am I pursuing now?

Month Eleven

Week Forty-four

"Find someone you can tell the truth to; we don't do this alone."

Over the twelve months when my life crashed around me, I shut myself off more and more from the people I knew. On those rare occasions when people who knew me asked how I was, I lied and told them I was fine. The truth was that I was isolated, desperate, and utterly without hope. I knew the end was near, and I didn't care; in fact, when it came I was actually relieved.

When I entered the program, my life became the antithesis of what it had been before. Rather than isolating, I went to meetings. Instead of eating alone, I went out with groups of people afterwards. And instead of lying about things being fine, I learned to speak my truth and tell people what was really going on with me.

Today I know that the only way I can stay comfortable in my own skin is by letting other people into my life and sharing with them what I'm going through. Alone, my head will still lie to me, but when I reach out to others and tell them honestly what I'm thinking, feeling or doing, that's when the miracle of recovery takes place.

Today I know the importance of finding someone you can tell the truth to, because we can't, and don't, do this alone.

Reflections:

How honest about my life was I before I entered recovery?

Had my world become small?

When I entered recovery, what was it like for me to participate in and attend meetings?

What was my experience like as I began to honestly tell others what was really happening in my life?

How does my head treat me when I'm alone today?

Do I regularly still tell people what is really going on with me?

Week Forty-five

"Try praying. Nothing pleases God more than hearing a strange voice."

This quote hit me on several levels. First, it reminded me of how often I forget to use one of the most powerful tools in my spiritual toolkit: Prayer. I was taught early on that praying is simply talking to God, and my repeated experience is that it works in so many ways. Each time I use it, I receive the peace, guidance, and strength I need to live life with grace and serenity.

This quote also reminds me that no matter how long it has been since I reached out to God, He is always waiting and happy to hear from me. I remember I learned this lesson early on in my recovery when I was angry with God and was guilty as I blamed and cursed Him. My sponsor told me that it didn't matter what I said to God - He was big enough to handle it - the important thing was that I was finally talking to God.

What this taught me is that God's love for me is unconditional. Knowing this enabled me to develop an open and honest dialogue that led to a loving and trusting relationship with my Higher Power. I grow and benefit from this relationship each time I remember to pray, and this quote reminds me that no matter how long it has been, God is always ready and happy to hear from me.

Reflections:

How often do I pray?

Do I ever stop to pray in the middle of the day?

What kind of results or feelings do I get when I do pray?

Have I ever been angry with God?

Have I ever been afraid that God might not like me when I'm angry with Him?

How do I deal with that today?

Week Forty-six

"Behaviors are like tennis rackets; if yours is broken, get a new one."

A woman at a meeting shared that behaviors are like tennis rackets. While a tennis racket works for a while – years, even - eventually the strings wear out, the grip comes apart, and after a while you have to get a new one. She said that for years she was using rackets of behavior long after they had stopped working. It was only after she "got a new racket" that her life improved.

When I was new to recovery, I had a lot of old, worn out rackets, too. What I didn't realize was that the reason my life wasn't working was because I kept trying to use them to achieve different results. When I spoke with my sponsor about it, he told me that unless I worked the steps and changed the way I thought and acted, the results in my life would stay the same.

Today, I'm much better at recognizing my old rackets of behaviors, and, thankfully, I'm more willing to try something different. Today when areas of my life aren't working, I know to look at my behavior, talk to someone in the program, and pray for guidance. Today, when my racket isn't working, I'm quick to get a new one.

Today I know that I can't win if I continue to play with an old racket.

Reflections:

How many rackets did I come into the program with?

What were some of the results of my refusing to let go of them?

How long did it take for me to recognize them as rackets?

What did it take for me to become willing to get new ones?

What do I do today if a new racket I use isn't working?

Do I reach out to people and my Higher Power often enough when I don't get my way?

Week Forty-seven

"People have the right not to recover."

The first time I heard this saying, I thought it was cruel and insensitive. I had been in Al-Anon about six months and was still convinced that I not only could help other people in my life recover, but that it was, in fact, my job to do so. Learning to detach with love was still foreign to me and the idea of allowing someone to destroy their life was unthinkable. When I asked my sponsor what to do he told me to look at my own experience.

As a double winner (in both programs), I knew firsthand how ineffective others were in trying to get me to see the dangers of my drinking and using. The more they tried to warn me or control my behavior, the more I resented and avoided them. In fact, their attempts had the opposite effect: They drove me to isolate and drink even more! In the end, what I learned to be true is what I've since heard in meetings a thousand times: Until we admit to our innermost selves that we're an alcoholic (or addict), we won't do the things we need to do to get and stay sober.

Over the years, one of the things that continues to baffle me is why some people recover and others - who so obviously need it and would benefit from it - don't. I've had to accept my powerlessness over others, but it's still hard to see those I care about ruin their lives. My sponsor once told me that I needed to respect someone's decision to drink themselves to death. That still sounds harsh, but there's a strange, sad truth to it.

It's a reminder that people have the right to not recover.

Reflections:

Do I have people in my life that need to be in recovery?

How do I feel when I read today's quote?

What has my experience been when I've tried to get others to stop drinking or using?

Do I still believe that somehow I can get someone to quit or control their disease?

Have I accepted my powerlessness over other people, places and things?

Do I respect other people's decisions to live their lives the way they choose?

Month Twelve

Week Forty-eight

"Wisdom is knowledge you learn after you know it all."

You couldn't tell me anything before I entered recovery because I knew it all. I had all the answers for my life, and I had all the answers for yours, too, and I was quick to tell you about it. As I've already said one of my favorite sayings back then was, "Those who think they know it all are really annoying to those of us who do!"

When I came into the program, I brought all my opinions into the rooms with me. At first I tried to do things my way and thought I had better answers than you. I mean, "Turn it over?" "Let go and let God?" That may work for you, but I was sure I knew better. 90 days later, though, I was drunk!

When I finally admitted that I didn't know how to stay sober, I became willing to admit that perhaps I didn't know everything after all. That was the moment I became teachable, and it was the moment I began to recover. The longer I'm in the program, the more I realize that many times what I think I know, just isn't so.

*Today I'm quick to admit that I don't have the answers, and when
I do I become open to the wisdom that lies beyond.*

Reflections:

Did I think I had all the answers before recovery?

If so, then why wasn't my life working?

When I entered the program, how open was I to the suggestions of others?

When did I finally become teachable?

What is the difference for me between knowledge and wisdom?

What do I have more of in my life today?

Week Forty-nine

"If you stay on the train long enough, the scenery will change."

Whenever I talk to a newcomer, I remember the insanity of early recovery. I used to talk in endless circles about my problems and about the people, places and things responsible for them. I went on and on about how I could never stop drinking, and I was convinced the program wouldn't work for me. I didn't believe it when people told me, "This too shall pass," but I was out of options, so I kept showing up hoping they were right.

It took many months of staying sober and working the program, but things did begin to change. I began feeling better physically, my head cleared, and I became open to a new way of living. As I took different actions, I got different results, and after a while my life improved. More importantly, I developed the perspective of recovery, and I learned, firsthand, that things do change as long as I'm willing to change first.

Today I know that I can only keep changing and keep growing if I stay on the train of recovery. No matter what the scenery looks like today (and sometimes it's not so pretty), as long as I continue to grow along spiritual lines, I know that it will change and things will get better. This has been my consistent and enduring experience, and I now live by and trust in the knowledge that:

If you stay on the train long enough, the scenery will definitely change.

Reflections:

How self-obsessed was I in early recovery?

Did I feel my problems and life were beyond salvation?

When did things begin to change for me?

At what point did I develop the "perspective of recovery?"

What happens to those who get off the train of recovery?

What am I doing to continue to grow along spiritual lines?

Week Fifty

"Don't take yourself so damn seriously!"

When I came into the program, everything was a big deal, and I was very serious. My finances, my future, my wrecked relationships - everything was overwhelming. I remember attending meetings and hearing the laughter and thinking, "What's so damn funny? The only reason we're here is because our lives suck!" It took me quite a while before I could join in with that laughter, and the moment I did my life began to change.

As I got further into the program, that sense of impending doom began to dissipate, and I felt like I could breathe again. The secrets and shame I had hidden for so long began to come out, and as I shared what was inside me with others, I began to feel lighter. I began to laugh more at myself and with others, and I finally began to feel human and a part of life again. Most of all, I started to realize what was truly important.

Today, I know that the future will take care of itself if I take care of today. I now have faith that there is a God working in my life, and that even if things don't go my way, that it's not only OK, it often turns out for the better. Today, money isn't as important as relationships, and the only things that really matters are health and sobriety.

Today I've learned to live life on life's terms and, most of all, not to take myself so damn seriously.

Reflections:

How serious was I when I was a newcomer?

How did I feel when I heard the laughter in the rooms?

When did I begin to join in with that laughter?

Am I still too serious at times?

What do I do to lighten up?

Have I figured out what is really important yet? If so, what is it?

Week Fifty-one

"You know you'll be back, so why don't you just stay?"

When I had 93 days of sobriety, I went out. I copped a resentment at my Wednesday night meeting because they ran out of ninety day chips, so I stormed out, went home and drank. I still remember the feelings of relief I had as I drank that big glass of port wine - I was off the program and no longer had to descend into the pit of shame the steps were leading me into. Even so, I also knew there was no other way to recover and that I would be back.

After several months of drinking and yet still going to meetings, I finally quit for good. Once again, I started working the program, all the while dreading the fourth step. When I got to it and starting making a list of resentments and my part in them, I truly felt I had descended into Hell and was sure that once my sins and secrets were revealed, I would be shunned, abandoned or even arrested.

What I found instead was amazing. Where I thought I would be alone, I found that people trudged the road with me, helped me, and even understood. Where I thought I would find the darkest parts of myself, I found my connection to my Higher Power. When I thought I'd be abandoned, I found a great fellowship and know now that I don't ever have to be alone again.

Today, I encourage others who want to go out to stay - you know you'll be back anyway.

Reflections:

How many times have I gone in and out of recovery?

At what point did I just surrender and stay?

Did I fear or dread the fourth step?

What was my experience like when I did it?

What gifts have I received now that I have been through the fifth step?

When people tell me they want to go out, what do I say to them?

Week Fifty-two

"The only thing we can take with us when we leave this world is what we gave away."

For years I thought the goal in life was to get as much stuff as I could. I measured my worth as a person by how much money I had in the bank, by how many books and CD's I had, and I spent endless hours shopping for expensive cars, hipper clothes and newer tech devices. I loved when the UPS truck came, and for a few hours I almost felt satisfied. I still remember, however, the moment I pressed the buy button on yet another Amazon.com order, and thought about the package arriving and putting the new, unread books on the shelf next to the other new, unread books. In that moment, I bottomed out.

When I was new in the program, I was told that if I wanted to feel better, then I had to get out of myself by being of service and by helping others. While I argued that cleaning coffee cups and helping in the kitchen couldn't have anything to do with my recovering or feeling better, I did what I was told. Eventually, I was instructed to sponsor and work with others. While I resented getting up early on Sunday mornings to meet with a newcomer before a meeting, I can tell you now that I always felt the deepest satisfaction and feeling of self-worth when I did. Finally I had found a way to fill the hole inside of me.

What I've learned in 14 years of recovery is that it's not about me. It's not about how much I earn, or how much I can get, or how much I have. Instead, it's only about how much I can give away. The truth in my life today is that I'm happiest when I seek to be of service. I'm less in fear when I'm thinking of others, and ultimately I know that the only thing that really matters now, and will matter forever, is how much I've packed into the stream of life. It's taken many years, but I finally understand the last line of the St. Francis prayer:

"It is by dying that one awakens to eternal life."

Reflections:

How did I measure my self-worth before recovery?

What did I use to try to fill the hole inside of me?

When I was new in the program, what kind of suggestions did I get?

What was my reaction to them?

How much time do I spend today thinking about myself, versus thinking of ways to be of service to others?

What am I packing into the stream of life today?

Michael Z

Michael Z lives and writes in Los Angeles, CA. A registered marriage and family therapist intern and spiritual counselor, he uses the Twelve Steps as a guide for spiritual, emotional and physical recovery. He shares his experience, strength and hope in meetings, conventions, and treatment centers around the world, working with both groups and individuals in helping them deepen their understanding and experience of the Twelve Step journey.

In addition to four volumes of Wisdom of the Rooms books, Michael still publishes weekly Wisdom Quotes and sayings each Monday and distributes them to an international subscriber base. You can sign up for free by visiting:

www.TheWisdomoftheRooms.com

Michael also leads workshops and retreats on the Twelve Steps, and he coaches individuals helping to empower them to lead richer and more creative lives. To learn more about his spiritual coaching or Modern Hero's Journey retreats, email him at:

MichaelZ@theWisdomoftheRooms.com

www.TheWisdomoftheRooms.com

Once again it has taken many dedicated people to bring this Wisdom of the Rooms, Volume Four book to you. To start with, I want to say a very special thank you to all of you on my Wisdom E-mail list who, throughout the year, have sent me your comments and stories of how these Wisdom quotes have affected you. Your E-mails have brought me so much inspiration. Just when I thought I couldn't write another quote, someone would send me something that gave me motivation to keep writing. Thank you all so very much.

I'd also like to thank my beautiful wife, Qi, for all the Sundays she would encourage me to write my quote while she filled the house with the wonderful smell of our Sunday dinner. I also want to thank you, honey, for all the work you put into this volume by reaching out for testimonials, following up on the foreword, and for the loving work you put into this book. Your constant support and unconditional love and encouragement, along with your honest and gentle suggestions, mean so very much to me. I love you.

Next I'd like to thank Jennie for her meticulous work on proofing the manuscript and for hand-delivering it to me when finished. You're the best, Jennie! I'd also like to thank Joe and Judy for the work they did on the foreword and for helping me pass the Wisdom on through the work that they do.

A great big thank you goes out to the team at Three Palms Press, and especially to my publisher, Jeb Blount, for taking on yet another of my books and setting the time aside to get it out in the world. I know it's been a busy year for you and I thank you so much for helping me get yet another Wisdom book out there to those who need and want it.

Lastly, I want to thank Bill and Bob, Co-founders of the Program and the wonderful fellowship it has engendered, where so many miracles take place. Their vision and dedication, and the legacy they left behind, continue to change lives and transform the world.

CPSIA information can be obtained at www.ICGtesting.com
Printed in the USA
LVOW07s1719200715

446911LV00002B/356/P